# Redeemed

## THROUGH PEACE

### AL C. EZRA

# Copyright

# Redeemed

## THROUGH PEACE

A book of reflection, Scripture, and restoration

by Al Ezra

Inspired by the Ruach Ha-Kodesh

*"Peace I leave with you—My peace I give to you."*

—John 14:27

# **Dedication**

To the weary soul,

the one who has wrestled in silence,

the one who has prayed in tears,

the one who has longed for stillness

but felt trapped in the storm—

this is for you.

To all who seek peace—

those who hunger for stillness in a restless world,

who long for clarity in the storm,

and who are willing to walk the narrow road of truth.

Peace is not far.

He is near.

May you be redeemed through peace,

restored by truth,

and rooted forever in the name of Jesus of Nazareth.

May your heart be anchored in the Prince of Peace.

May your name be written.

May your feet find the path that leads home.


Peace, to you!

AL EZRA

Inspired by The Book of Ezra

# Table of Contents

## Chapter 6

## Chapter 7

## Closing Words

# Introduction

This book is a compilation of six years of prayer, study, spiritual battle, and revelation. It was not written in the aftermath of suffering, but in the midst of ongoing oppression. This was a season marked by the enemy's relentless attacks on me and my family. Yet in the middle of that fire, the peace of the Lord never failed. His promises never broke.

Out of that fiery furnace came these priceless truths of how to find true peace that I want to share with you.

## What does it mean to be Redeemed through Peace?

The path begins and ends with Jesus of Nazareth, the Prince of Peace.

> *For a child will be born for us, a son will be given to us, and the government will be on his shoulders. He will be named Wonderful Counselor, Mighty God, Eternal Father, Prince of Peace.*
>
> —Isaiah 9:6 (CSB)

To be redeemed means to be purchased back, restored, and made whole by the finished work of the cross. Jesus shed His blood as the final, perfect sacrifice, not for the righteous, but for ALL who believe. It is His redemption, and it is His peace.

> *In him we have redemption through his blood, the forgiveness of our trespasses, according to the riches of his grace.*
>
> —Ephesians 1:7 (CSB)

> *But Christ has appeared as a high priest of the good things that have come. In the greater and more perfect tabernacle not made with hands, he entered the most holy place once for all time, not by the blood of goats and calves, but by his own blood, having obtained eternal redemption.*
>
> —Hebrews 9:11–12 (CSB)

This peace cannot be earned. It is neither the result of religious striving, nor is it based on our human works.

> *For you are saved by grace through faith, and this is not from yourselves; it is God's gift not from works, so that no one can boast.*
>
> —Ephesians 2:8-9 (CSB)

Redemption through peace is not man reaching up to the Infinite. It is the Infinite reaching down to man. It is the Most High calling us back into fellowship with Himself.

> *But God proves his own love for us in that while we were still sinners, Christ died for us.*
>
> —Romans 5:8 (CSB)

> *"No one has greater love than this: to lay down his life for his friends."*
>
> —John 15:13 (CSB)

To be redeemed through peace is to have an eternal perspective in a temporal world. It is to understand that the cross is not only our rescue. It is our rest.

> *Jesus said to her, "I am the resurrection and the life. The one who believes in me, even if he dies, will live. Everyone who lives and believes in me will never die. Do you believe this?"*
>
> —John 11:25-26 (CSB)

This book opens up the invitation of Yeshua to you His beloved:

- To understand the power of His redemption
- To believe on the finished work of the cross, and live
- To meet with the Prince of Peace
- To take on the role of peacemaker
- To walk in the power of the Holy Spirit
- To live in freedom from fear

He has already done the work.

He is our Redeemer.

He is our Peace.

And His peace gives us shalom, wholeness, stillness, and strength through the love that laid down everything for us.

> *"Peace I leave with you. My peace I give to you. I do not give to you as the world gives. Don't let your heart be troubled or fearful."*
>
> —John 14:27 (CSB)

Peace, to you! (*Shalom Aleichem!*)

**Al C. Ezra**

# Chapter 1

# The Path to Peace

> *"Peace I leave with you; My peace I give to you—not as the world gives do I give to you. Do not let your heart be troubled or afraid."*
>
> —John 14:27

There is a peace the world promises—one that rests in circumstances that bend with the news cycle, and falters with the economy. Then there is the peace that Yeshua (Jesus) gives. It is a different kind of peace entirely—one that does not come from man, but from God alone. It cannot be explained by logic or maintained through personal strength. It is a gift, born in the heart of the Savior and given freely to all who believe.

The Hebrew word for *peace* is *shalom*. *Shalom* means more than the absence of conflict. This peace speaks of wholeness, completion, soundness, and harmony with God. To be redeemed through peace means to be made whole through the finished work of the cross, through the blood of Jesus who reconciled us to the Father.

But how do we walk this path? What does it look like to live in this peace—not just as an idea, but as a way of life?

## A Heart Anchored in Trust

Isaiah 26:3 gives this promise,

> *You keep in Him perfect peace one whose mind is stayed on You, because he trusts in You.*

Peace begins in the heart and in the mind. It is the result of trust. If our minds are fixed on the chaos of the world, fear will dominate. But if our minds are fixed on the promises of God, peace will prevail.

The path to peace requires focus—an intentional turning of the eyes toward heaven, even when everything around you is turbulent. It's the kind of peace Daniel had in the lions' den, the kind the disciples saw in Jesus asleep on a storm-tossed boat. The winds did not disturb Him, because His peace was not tied to His surroundings. It came from His communion with the Father.

## The Peace that Comes through Faith

We receive that peace when we trust. Romans 5:1 declares:

> *Therefore, having been made righteous by trusting, we have shalom with God through our Lord Yeshua the Messiah.*

This is the foundation of all peace: righteousness by faith. When we try to earn peace by our own efforts, we fail. But when we trust in the finished work of Messiah—who bore our sins and conquered death—we are justified, made right before God, and ushered into His peace.

This peace is not emotional; it is eternal, and covenantal. We were once enemies of God, bound by sin and rebellion. But through faith in Yeshua, we are reconciled, adopted, and welcomed into His rest.

## The Peace that Guards and Governs

Philippians 4:6-7 tells us:

> *Do not be anxious about anything—but in everything, by prayer and petition with thanksgiving, let your requests be made known to God. And the shalom of God, which surpasses all understanding, will guard your hearts and your minds in Messiah Yeshua.*

The path to peace is paved with prayer. We are not called to carry every burden or solve every problem. We are called to cast our cares upon Him. Prayer is not simply about asking—it is about laying down our anxiety in exchange for His peace.

The promise here is astounding: God's peace will guard our hearts and minds. Like a fortress, like a shield, His peace becomes our protection. In a world full of turmoil, it is this peace that stands watch over us.

## Loving His Word, Loving His Peace

Psalm 119:165 reminds us:

> *Great peace have they who love Your Torah, and nothing causes them to stumble.*

Loving the Word of God leads to deep peace. Scripture renews our minds and reminds us who we are, whose we are, and where our hope lies. In a world filled with deception, truth brings freedom. And freedom brings peace.

The Word of God becomes our compass. It teaches us how to respond, how to walk in obedience, how to release bitterness, and how to forgive. When we live according to His instructions, we experience peace that surpasses every circumstance.

## Let Peace Rule

Paul writes in Colossians 3:15:

> Let the **shalom** of Messiah rule in your hearts—to this **shalom** you were surely called in one body. Also be thankful.

Do you know where Paul was at the time of writing this letter? In a Roman jail!

So we see that peace is not just something we feel—it is something we let rule. That means it's a decision. When conflict comes, when fear whispers, when discouragement creeps in, we can say, "No, I will let peace rule. I will not give in to fear."

This ruling peace is connected to unity in the body of Messiah. We are called to peace not only to the outside world but among one another. Peace is relational. The peace we receive from God, we are meant to extend to others. This is how the world will know we are His disciples—'By our love one for another.'

## A Narrow Path, But a Sure One

The way to peace is not the popular well-trodden path. It may require letting go of offense. It may require silence when provoked. It may mean blessing those who curse you, loving those who betrayed you, and trusting God when your flesh wants revenge. But it is a sure path. A strong path. A holy path.

Jesus said, "*Blessed are the peacemakers*." He didn't say, "Blessed are the peacekeepers." There is a difference. A peacekeeper avoids conflict to keep things quiet. A peacemaker *enters* conflict to bring restoration.

Peacemakers are bold. Peacemakers carry the heart of God.

To walk this path is to walk with Jesus—to follow His steps from Gethsemane to Calvary and into the garden of Resurrection. Peace does not mean living a painless life, but a purposeful one. It means being held in the hand of the Father, even when the world is tottering.

## Final Thought

The peace that Yeshua offers is not fleeting. It does not leave when the storm begins. No, it deepens. It grows. It testifies.

And it redeems.

Peace is not just the outcome of redemption—it is a path that leads us there. It's a journey that transforms us along the way. When we walk in the peace of Christ, we are walking home—back to the Father, back to truth, back to life.

Will you take the first step?

# Chapter 2

# Peace in the Midst of Conflict

> *"You will keep in perfect peace those whose minds are steadfast, because they trust in you.*
>
> —Isaiah 26:3 (NIV)

Throughout the Scriptures, we encounter men and women whose lives were anything but peaceful in the worldly sense. Yet their trust in God anchored them in deep, abiding shalom. These were not people free from conflict, but people who found peace in the midst of it.

To understand the journey of peace, we must walk in the footsteps of those who went before us. These men and women, by faith and obedience, stepped into the calm center of God's promises, even while the storms of life raged around them.

## Moses: Peace in the Presence of God

Moses' life began with danger. Hidden in a basket and floated down the Nile, his destiny was marked from the beginning by deliverance. Raised in Pharaoh's court, yet Hebrew by birth, Moses' conflict with an Egyptian led him to flee into the wilderness—a place where many hide in exile, but where Moses found peace.

It was there, in the quiet of Horeb, that Moses encountered the voice of God in the burning bush. No longer striving in his own strength, he learned to listen. He learned that peace comes from walking in God's calling, even when the path is unknown.

When he stood before Pharaoh, it wasn't in his own authority. It was in obedience. And when the Red Sea split and the Israelites crossed over, it was not because Moses fought with weapons, but because he lifted his staff in faith.

The wilderness became a place of revelation, and the tent of meeting a place of intimacy. Moses said to God, "*If Your Presence does not go with us, do not send us up from here!*" (Exodus 33:15). He understood that peace is not a place—it's a Person. Where God is, there is peace.

## Elijah: Peace Beyond the Fire

Elijah's story is one of intensity. He called down fire from heaven to confront the false prophets of Baal, and challenge the king. Yet even after great victory, he found himself running in fear. He hid in a cave, a broken man.

There, on Mount Horeb, God revealed something essential about peace. It didn't come through the wind. It didn't come through the earthquake. It didn't even come through the fire. It came in a still, small voice.

God wasn't finished with Elijah—He was just changing the way Elijah listened. The lesson was simple but profound: Peace does not always roar. Sometimes it whispers. And if you listen carefully, you'll hear God in the silence.

Elijah emerged with renewed purpose. The circumstances had not changed, but his spirit had been quieted by the presence of God. In that stillness, he was recommissioned—and from that place of peace, he continued his mission.

## Ruth: Peace through Loyalty and Love

Ruth's journey to peace began in loss. Recently widowed, this young Moabite woman was childless. She had no inheritance, no security, and no future in the natural sense. Yet she clung to her mother-in-law Naomi and embraced her God saying, "*Your people will be my people, and your God my God*" (Ruth 1:16).

Her peace was not inherited—it was chosen. She declared her allegiance to the God of Naomi, the God of Israel, and took shelter under His wings. She worked in the grain fields of Boaz, humble and faithful, trusting in a provision she could not yet see.

And it came. Redemption came. Not just for Ruth, but for the lineage of David, that ultimately led to the Messiah. Ruth's faith and loyalty brought her into covenant with God. And that covenant led her to peace—not just for her own soul, but for generations to come.

**Peace Is a Pattern**

Each of these stories teaches us something about peace:

- Moses teaches us that peace comes through presence—being close to God.
- Elijah shows us that peace is not found in noise and activity, but in intimacy and stillness.
- Ruth reveals that peace is the reward of loyalty, even when all is lost.

None of them had an easy path. None of them had control over their circumstances. But they all trusted in the God who does not change. And in doing so, they found peace.

# The Peace that Comes through Obedience

There is a peace that can only be accessed through obedience. We see this in the story of Joshua, who followed Moses and was called to lead Israel into the Promised Land. Over and over again, God told him, "*Be strong and courageous*"—not because Joshua would not face battles, but because God promised to be with him.

In every step of obedience, peace followed. The walls of Jericho fell not through war, but through worship. The land was taken not through compromise, but through consecration.

Obedience aligns us with the heart of God, and alignment produces peace. It is when we resist God that we become restless. But when we surrender, we find that even in warfare, there is a holy rest.

> *The work of righteousness will be peace, and the effect of righteousness, quietness and assurance forever.*
>
> —Isaiah 32:17

## Peace through the Valley

Psalm 23 offers perhaps the most beloved image of peace in the Bible:

> *Even though I walk through the valley of the shadow of death, I will fear no evil, for You are with me.*

David, the shepherd-king, knew the valley well. He knew betrayal, warfare, and personal failure. But he also knew this: Peace is not the absence of shadows. It is the presence of the Shepherd.

The valley becomes an encounter when the Lord steps in. The shadows do not overcome us because His rod and staff comfort us. And in the place where the valley is darkest, we find a table—a place of feasting, even in the presence of enemies.

That is peace.

## Jesus in the Stories

What ties all these stories together is that they point to Jesus, the epitome of peace. He is the better Moses—our Deliverer. He is the still small voice that called Elijah. He is the Redeemer greater than Boaz. He is the Shepherd David sang of. In every narrative, He is present.

And Jesus does not just offer peace—He is peace. All those who trust in Him, who walk in His ways, will find that their story, too, becomes a narrative of peace.

## Closing Reflection

The Word of God is not just a history book, it's a mirror. As you read these stories, you may find pieces of your own life woven into the journey: the wilderness, the cave, the threshing floor, the valley. More than locations, they are invitations—invitations to encounter the God of peace.

The path has been walked before. Others have trusted, others have endured, others have obeyed. And they found Him faithful.

So can you.

# Chapter 3

# Who are the Peacemakers?

*"Blessed are the peacemakers, for they shall be called sons of God."*

—Matthew 5:9

The voice that echoed across the hills of Galilee was not like any other. It came with no sword, no threat, no chains. It did not stir rebellion or political uprising. Yet it had the power to break through pride, transform hearts, and bring down God's kingdom to earth.

That voice belonged to Yeshua, the Prince of Peace.

He sat down, as a rabbi would, and spoke not to the powerful, but to the poor in spirit—the hungry, the ones who had ears to hear. His words were radical—not because they promised comfort, but because they redefined blessing altogether. And in the midst of this divine teaching came a call unlike any other:

*"Blessed are the peacemakers."*

Not the peace-lovers. Not the peacekeepers. But the peacemakers.

## The Heart of a Peacemaker

To be a peacemaker is to be like God. It is to enter chaos not with force, but with truth. It is to sow calm where there is fury, to reconcile what was broken. It is to carry heaven's agenda into earth's divisions. And it is costly.

The peacemaker is not passive. The peacemaker is not blind. They see the conflict clearly—and step into it anyway. They speak the truth in love. They forgive before they are asked. They tear down the wall that others would rather leave separating one from the other.

And Jesus says they are blessed. Why? Because peacemakers reveal the Father. They bear His likeness. They walk in His ways. When you see a true peacemaker, you are seeing the nature of God.

## Peace, Not Compromise

The peace of Jesus is not political, superficial, or manipulative. It is not the peace that the world gives (John 14:27). It is not simply the absence of strife. Rather, it is the presence of righteousness.

As it says in James 3:17-18:

> *But the wisdom that is from above is first pure, then peaceable, gentle, open to reason, full of mercy and good fruits, without partiality and without hypocrisy. And the fruit of righteousness is sown in shalom by those who make shalom.*

Peacemaking does not mean ignoring sin. It's means confronting it with grace. Peacemakers do not sweep injustice under the rug. They call it out—but with humility, not rage, with healing, not harm. They live at a higher wisdom that reflects the heart of heaven.

## Jesus, the Perfect Peacemaker

Everything Jesus did was rooted in peace. He didn't come to condemn the world but to save it (John 3:17). When the woman caught in adultery was thrown before Him, He did not join the accusers. He stooped low. He disarmed the mob with one sentence, "*Let him who is without sin among you, cast the first stone at her*" (John 8:7 KJV), and gave her grace to begin again.

When He approached Zacchaeus, the dishonest tax collector, He didn't shame him in public. He simply said, "*Come down, for I must stay at your house today.*" That one invitation brought repentance and restoration.

When His disciples argued about who was greatest, He taught them that greatness is found in humility, in serving others.

And when He was betrayed, beaten, and crucified—He said, "*Father, forgive them.*"

This is what a peacemaker looks like.

## Peace as a Mission

Peacemaker are not merely blessed—they are sent. Paul writes in Romans 10:15,

> *How beautiful are the feet of those who proclaim good news of good things!*

The Gospel itself is a message of peace—between God and man, and between man and his brother. To carry this Gospel is to bring the terms of peace to a world at war.

This is our mission: to reconcile, to redeem, to restore.

As Paul says in 2 Corinthians 5:18-19:

> *Now all these things are from God, who reconciled us to Himself through Messiah and gave us the ministry of reconciliation. That is, in Messiah God was reconciling the world to Himself, not counting their trespasses against them; and He has entrusted the message of reconciliation to us.*

You and I have been given this ministry. It is not optional. It is the calling of every believer—to be an ambassador of peace in a world full of division.

# A Kingdom Culture

Many see the Sermon on the Mount as a lecture about being good and obeying the law. Far from it! It is one of the most radical proclamations ever made. It is a blueprint for Kingdom life. It's a culture that runs counter to the values of the world.

- The world says: defend your rights. Jesus says: turn the other cheek.
- The world says: seek revenge. Jesus says: bless those who curse you.
- The world says: accumulate wealth. Jesus says: store treasure in heaven.
- The world exalts the proud and mighty. Jesus exalts the meek.

No wonder peacemakers are misunderstood! They are mocked. They are accused of being weak. But in the eyes of the King, they are sons and daughters of the Most High. They are royalty. They are reflections of the One who left heaven to make peace on earth.

## The Cost of Peacemaking

Peacemaking is costly because it requires us to die to self. To give up our need to be right. To forgive when it hurts. To risk being misunderstood. But it's worth it—because the reward is eternal. And even now on earth, you have a peace that the world cannot give.

But even peacemakers are not immune. Jesus warned His followers that persecution would come. In fact, they may suffer more. But He also said:

*"Rejoice and be glad, for your reward in heaven is great."*

—Matthew 5:12

He didn't promise that peacemakers would always be liked. He promised they would be blessed. Not just someday—but now. They walk in the shalom of God. They live in harmony with heaven.

## How to Be a Peacemaker

1.  Start in your heart. Ask the Holy Spirit to show you any area of unrest, resentment, or bitterness. Peace begins within.

2.  Speak the truth in love. Don't avoid hard conversations—but have them with gentleness and grace.

3.  Forgive quickly. Don't give the enemy a foothold. Let go. Release. Bless those who have wronged you.

4.  Pray for your enemies. Jesus commanded this not just for their sake, but for ours. Prayer changes hearts—starting with ours.

5.  Be intentional. Look for opportunities to bring unity. Be the bridge. Break the cycle of offense.

## Closing Thought

Peacemakers are not born. They are formed. Formed through surrender, through prayer, through the Word, through intimacy with the Father.

And every time you choose peace, every time you choose to reflect His nature instead of your flesh, you move deeper into your calling as a child of God.

Blessed are you, peacemaker! You bear His name.

# Chapter 4

# From Brokenness to Redemption

*Let the redeemed of ADONAI say so—whom He redeemed from the hand of the foe.*

—Psalm 107:2

Redemption is not a one-time act. It is a divine rhythm that echoes through every page of Scripture. It is the melody of mercy, the answer to despair, and the bridge that leads us back to peace.

From Genesis to Revelation, we are introduced to broken people in desperate need of restoration. And in every case—when they turn to the Lord—they find not just rescue, but shalom. They find a peace that mends what was lost, heals what was wounded, and secures what was threatened.

This chapter traces the footsteps of redemption through the Scriptures, revealing that peace is not just a result of salvation—it is a sign of it.

## Joseph: From the Pit to Peace

Joseph's story begins with betrayal. Sold by his brothers, falsely accused, imprisoned without cause—his path was littered with injustice. And yet, we see no bitterness in his response. He does not seek revenge. Instead, he says to those same brothers who wronged him:

*"You meant evil against me, but God meant it for good."*

—Genesis 50:20

Joseph's heart had been redeemed long before he saw his circumstances change. While he waited in prison, God was working in him. And when promotion came, he used his power not for retribution but for reconciliation.

That is the fruit of redemption: peace with the past, mercy for others, and clarity of purpose.

## David: Peace After Repentance

David was a man after God's own heart. But he also sinned grievously—taking Bathsheba, murdering her husband, and concealing his guilt. His peace was shattered. He later wrote:

> *When I kept silent, my bones became brittle through my groaning all day long.*
>
> —Psalm 32:3

But when he confessed, something shifted. The weight lifted. The peace returned. Not because the consequences vanished, but because the fellowship with God was restored.

David's redemption teaches us this: confession leads to cleansing, and cleansing leads to peace. God does not redeem to shame us—He redeems to heal us.

## The Woman at the Well: Peace in Identity

In John 4, we meet a woman coming to the well at noon—an hour when most avoided the sun, but she was avoiding people. Her past was marked by broken relationships and failed hopes. She was a Samaritan—despised by the Jews. Yet Jesus, a Jewish rabbi, speaks directly to her:

*"If you knew the gift of God... you would have asked Him, and He would have given you living water."*

— John 4:10

In one conversation, He reveals her wounds, her need, and her future. And she leaves her jar behind—not because she forgot it, but because she found what she was really thirsting for.

Redemption redefines our identity. She was no longer the outcast. She became the messenger. And through her testimony, others came to believe.

## Peter: Peace After Denial

Peter was bold—until he wasn't. He walked on water, declared Jesus to be the Messiah, swore he would never fall away. But when the rooster crowed, he remembered. He had denied the One he loved.

And yet, after the resurrection, Jesus seeks him out—not to scold, but to restore.

*"Simon, son of John, do you love Me?"*

—John 21:17

Three times He asks. Three times Peter says yes. And three times Jesus recommissions him: *"Feed My sheep."*

Redemption doesn't just restore relationship—it reassigns purpose. Peter went on to become a rock in the early Church. His peace came not from perfection, but from forgiveness.

## Paul: Peace from a New Life

Once called Saul, he hunted the followers of Jesus with religious zeal like no other. He believed he was doing God's work. But on the road to Damascus, he was confronted by the very One he persecuted.

*"Saul, Saul, why are you persecuting Me?"*

—Acts 9:4

That encounter changed everything. Blinded for three days, ministered to by Ananias, then filled with the Holy Spirit, Saul became Paul—a new name for a new mission. The persecutor became the preacher. The violent man became a vessel of peace.

Paul would later write:

*Therefore, if anyone is in Messiah, he is a new creation. The old things have passed away; behold, all things have become new.*

—2 Corinthians 5:17

**Peace comes when you realize you don't have to be who you used to be.**

## The Pattern of Redemption

Across these stories, we see the same thread:

- Joseph: Redemption from injustice
- David: Redemption from sin and guilt
- The Samaritan woman: Redemption from shame

> ⋛ Peter: Redemption from failure

> ⋛ Paul: Redemption from blind hatred

In each case, peace follows redemption. Not as a reward for good behavior, but as a sign of restored relationship with God.

Redemption is not earned—it is received. It is the result of God's mercy meeting man's need. And it always leads to peace.

## Your Story, Too

Perhaps you see yourself in any one of these stories.

Maybe more.

Maybe you, like Joseph, have suffered injustice. Or like David, you carry guilt. Perhaps you've been rejected like the woman at the well. Or failed publicly, like Peter. Or maybe, like Paul, you've been running in the wrong direction.

The good news is this: redemption is still available. The same God who met them will meet you. The same peace they received is promised to you.

*"Come now, let's settle this," says the LORD. "Though your sins are like scarlet, I will make them as white as snow. Though they are red like crimson, I will make them as white as wool."*

—Isaiah 1:18

## Closing Reflection

Redemption involves transformation. It turns prisons into palaces. Ashes into beauty. Regret into testimony. It makes the unclean clean, the unworthy accepted, the restless calm.

And that peace is not momentary—it is eternal. As it says in Romans 5:1:

> *Therefore, having been made righteous by trusting, we have shalom with God through our Lord Yeshua the Messiah.*

You have been redeemed through peace. And that peace is your inheritance.

# Chapter 5:

## Jesus as the Prince of Peace

> *For a child will be born to us, a son will be given to us... and His Name will be called... Prince of Peace.*

> —Isaiah 9:5-6

When Isaiah prophesied about the coming Messiah, he used titles that would resound through eternity: Wonderful Counselor, Mighty God, Everlasting Father, and Prince of Peace. No name was accidental. Each one reveals the nature of the Messiah. But perhaps none is more needed in our time than this: Prince of Peace.

Jesus did not come to start a religion. He came to bring reconciliation between heaven and earth. He came to destroy hostility, both seen and unseen. He came not just to preach peace, but to be peace—peace incarnate, peace crucified, peace risen.

He did not ride in on a war horse. He came in lowly, riding on a donkey. He did not call for the sword in Gethsemane. He healed the one who was struck. At every turn, He modeled the way of peace—through humility, surrender, truth, and love.

This chapter unveils the Prince of Peace, not as a concept, but as a King whose peace still transforms lives today.

## Peace Announced at His Birth

From the beginning, His life was marked by peace. When the angels appeared to the shepherds in the field, they declared:

> *"Glory to God in the highest, and on earth shalom to men of good will."*

> —Luke 2:14

This was a powerful declaration. A new age had dawned. The silence between God and man was broken. A child had been born—not merely to bring peace, but to become the vessel of it.

He would grow in wisdom and stature, but even as a child, He carried the weight of heaven's promise.

## Peace in His Presence

Everywhere Jesus went, peace followed.

- He spoke to the wind and waves: "*Peace, be still!*"—Mark 4:39
- He spoke to the woman with the issue of blood: "*Daughter, your faith has made you well. Go in shalom.*" —Luke 8:48
- He wept over Jerusalem: "*If only you had recognized this day the things that lead to shalom!*" —Luke 19:42

His peace was not passive. It wasn't the absence of conflict—it was the presence of divine authority. When Jesus entered a situation, anxiety had to flee. Demons trembled. The sick were healed. The broken were restored.

His peace carried weight because it came from His identity. He was not a man trying to calm storms, He was the Creator of the seas, the One who set the boundaries of the oceans. And in Him, all things held together.

## Peace Through the Cross

The true depth of Jesus' peace was revealed not in His miracles, but in His suffering.

Isaiah 53:5 (NIV) says:

> *The punishment that brought us peace was upon Him, and by His wounds we are healed.*

Peace came at a price. The Prince of Peace wore a crown of thorns. He was pierced for our transgressions, crushed for our iniquities. His body was broken so ours could be made whole. The cross is where the war ended between man and God.

Colossians 1:19-20 says:

> *For God was pleased to have all His fullness dwell in Him, and through Him to reconcile all things to Himself... making peace through the blood of His cross.*

This peace is not shallow. It is blood-stained. It is anchored in justice. Sin had to be dealt with. And Jesus, out of love, became the sin offering. He is our Passover. Passover was the final atonement for all of our sins through the blood of the Lamb 🐑. That is Yeshua Himself.

## Peace that Passes Understanding

After His resurrection, Jesus appeared to His disciples—men who had abandoned Him, denied Him, and feared for their lives. And the first words out of His mouth were not condemnation. They were:

> *"Peace be with you."*
>
> —John 20:19

He spoke peace to men who had none. And it wasn't just words—it was power. His presence calmed their trembling hearts. His breath gave them the Spirit. His wounds proved that redemption was real.

This is the peace that Paul later describes in Philippians 4:7:

> *And the **shalom** of God, which surpasses all understanding, will guard your hearts and your minds in Messiah **Yeshua**.*

It's not a peace that makes sense in the natural. It's a peace that carries you through loss, rejection, pain, and persecution. It is sustained not by your strength, but by your union with the Prince of Peace.

## Peace Between Jew and Gentile

Yeshua also came to remove the dividing wall between people. Ephesians 2:14 (ESV) says:

> *For he himself is our peace, who has made us both one and has broken down in his flesh the dividing wall of hostility.*

Through His body, He reconciled Jew and Gentile, male and female, slave and free. In His Kingdom, there is no superiority—only unity. The peace of Jesus isn't just personal, it's societal. It heals racial wounds, tribal divisions, generational hatred. It brings the estranged into family, the outsider into covenant.

Only Jesus can do this. Governments legislate it. Movements attempt it. But only Messiah is peace.

**Our Inheritance of Peace**

As His followers, peace is our inheritance. In John 14:27, Jesus said:

> *"Shalom I leave you, My shalom I give to you; but not as the world gives! Do not let your heart be troubled or afraid."*

This is not borrowed peace. It's His peace. And He gives it to us—freely, permanently, and powerfully.

We are not called to live anxious, agitated, or afraid. We are called to live anchored. Even in tribulation,

Jesus says:

> *"In this world you will have trouble. But take heart! I have overcome the world."*
>
> —John 16:33

# Closing Reflection

The world is longing for peace. It looks for it in politics, in possessions, in human relationships—but never finds it. Because true peace isn't found in a system. It's found in a Savior.

Jesus is the Prince of Peace. He doesn't just bring calm—He brings reconciliation. He doesn't just offer stillness—He offers salvation. His peace reaches deeper than your pain, lasts longer than your trial, and speaks louder than your fear.

He is your peace—yesterday, today, and forever.

# Chapter 6:

# Living in the Spirit

> *But the fruit of the Ruach is love, joy, peace, patience, kindness, goodness, faithfulness, gentleness, and self-control.*
>
> —Galatians 5:22–23

Peace is not a personality trait—it is spiritual fruit. It does not originate from temperament, upbringing, or environment. It flows from the inner life of the believer—specifically from the presence of the *Ruach Ha-Kodesh*, the Holy Spirit, dwelling within.

The world teaches us to chase peace through stillness or separation, silence or success. But true, lasting, supernatural peace comes only by walking with the Spirit—daily, intentionally, and intimately.

The Spirit is not a concept. He is a Person. He is the third person of the Trinity God. And when we yield to Him, He produces fruit in our lives—fruit we cannot manufacture on our own. Among these is peace. And not just peace with God, but peace within ourselves and with others.

## The Spirit Bears What the Flesh Cannot

Galatians 5:17 reminds us that the flesh and the Spirit are at war with each other:

> *For the flesh sets its desire against the **Ruach**, but the **Ruach** sets its desire against the flesh—for these are in opposition to one another.*

You cannot walk in both the flesh and the Spirit. One always leads. The fruit of the flesh is obvious—strife, jealousy, anxiety, rage. But when the Spirit leads, peace begins to take root. It becomes evident. It softens your tone. It quiets your soul. It changes the atmosphere of your home.

The peace of the Spirit is not reactive. It is rooted. It does not come and go like emotions. It remains.

## Abide, and Peace Will Grow

Jesus said in John 15:4-5:

*"Abide in Me, and I will abide in you. The branch cannot itself produce fruit unless it abides on the vine ... apart from Me, you can do nothing."*

The fruit of peace grows where there is connection. If we're disconnected from the presence of God, our peace will wither. But if we stay rooted in Him—through prayer, worship, the Word, and obedience—peace will flourish.

It doesn't mean trials won't come. But it does mean we won't be moved by them. We won't because we are anchored.

Think of a tree planted by the river. Even in drought, it bears fruit. Why? Because its roots are deep. So is it with the believer who abides in the Spirit.

## The Spirit Calms the Storm Within

In Mark 4:39, Jesus rebuked the storm with the words, *"Peace, be still."* But first, He rebuked His disciples:

*"Why are you afraid? Even now you have no faith?"*

Fear is the enemy of peace. And fear grows where faith is absent.

The Holy Spirit builds faith. He reminds us who God is, what He has promised, and how He has been faithful before. He teaches us to trust in things unseen and hoped for.

When the Spirit is active in your life, panic loses its grip. The inner storm begins to still. You can hear the whisper of peace again. Remember, you are not alone. You are not abandoned, you are carried by Him.

## Walking in the Spirit Daily

Living in the Spirit is not mystical. It is practical. It looks like this:

- Starting your day in prayer
- Listening for God's voice in quiet moments
- Choosing love over asserting your rights
- Forgiving quickly
- Holding your tongue when tempted to lash out
- Trusting God when you don't understand

These are the steps of peace. And as you walk them, you begin to see transformation. Old habits lose power. Old triggers stop controlling you. The Spirit is forming peace within you.

Romans 8:6 says:

> For the mindset of the flesh is death, but the mindset of the **Ruach** is life and **shalom**.

To walk in peace, we must think peace. And to think peace, we must set our minds on the Spirit.

**Let Peace Rule**

Colossians 3:15 says:

> *Let the shalom of Messiah rule in your hearts—to this shalom you were surely called in one body. Also be thankful.*

The word "rule" here is from the Greek *brabeuó*—just like an umpire, deciding on the outcome of a match. In other words, peace is meant to guide your decisions. When you're unsure, ask: "Do I have peace from the Spirit?"

If not, wait. Don't force it. When the Spirit leads, peace follows.

And notice—this peace is communal—"One body." The Spirit does not just produce peace for you, but through you. You become a carrier of peace to your family, your community, your church. The fruit you bear feeds others.

## The Spirit's Witness of Peace

Isaiah 32:17 gives this beautiful promise:

> *The result of righteousness will be shalom and the effect of righteousness will be quietness and trust forever.*

When the Holy Spirit convicts us to walk rightly—to forgive, to surrender, to speak truth—He is not just leading us away from sin. He is leading us into peace.

The result of righteousness goes beyond holiness—it is stillness. Quietness of soul. A settled heart. A mind at rest.

The Spirit of God bears witness to our spirit—not only are we saved, we are seated in heavenly places. We are citizens of a kingdom that cannot be shaken.

And that knowledge gives peace.

## The Peace that Makes No Sense

Philippians 4:7 says:

> And the **shalom** of God, which surpasses all understanding, will guard your hearts and your minds in Messiah **Yeshua**.

This peace is beyond intellect. It's not logical. It doesn't depend on your bank account, your diagnosis, or your circumstances.

It is supernatural. And it stands guard. Like a sentry posted outside your heart, it turns away the arrows of fear and the daggers of doubt.

This is not peace from a system. This is peace from the Spirit. And it's yours—if you abide.

## Closing Reflection

Living in the Spirit is not just about power. It's about peace.

You may not see visions or hear thunder from heaven every day. But if your heart is still when it used to be anxious ... if your reactions are soft when they used to be sharp ... if your mind is quiet when it used to spin ... then you are bearing the fruit of peace.

Let Him do His work in you. Stay connected. Trust the process. Yield to the gentle guidance of the Ruach.

Because when you live in the Spirit—you live in peace.

# Chapter 7:

# Freedom from Fear

*For God has not given us a spirit of fear, but of power and love and of a sound mind. —2 Timothy 1:7 (NKJV)*

Fear is not an emotion—it is a spirit. And it does not come from G-d.

It is the weapon the enemy wields most efficiently. Fear enters quietly, wearing the mask of wisdom or caution, but its goal is always the same: to paralyze, deceive, and imprison. It will make you question your calling, delay your obedience, and convince you that G-d's promises won't come through.

But fear is a lie of the enemy. And every lie of the enemy falls powerless at the feet of truth.

You see the cross didn't just forgive your sin—it disarmed your enemy. Fear has no legal authority over a believer who is standing in the finished work of Messiah. As Yeshua said, "*It is finished!*" so has the battle already been won.

You do not fight for victory—you fight from a place of victory. You are more than a Conqueror.

# 1. Authority Has Been Given

In Luke 10:19, Jesus declared:

*"Behold, I have given you authority to trample upon serpents and scorpions, and over all the power of the enemy; nothing will harm you."*

These are not literally "serpents" and "scorpions." They represent sickness, oppression, doubt or fear and all the devices of the enemy. The good news is that we now have power over all of them. The authority once stolen in Eden has been restored through the Son of Man. And that authority has been handed to the sons and daughters of G-d.

It is not rooted in feelings, titles, or experiences. It is rooted in Him.

You don't have to be fearless to take authority—you just have to be faithful. Fear may knock, but you don't have to open the door. You've been given the keys of the Kingdom. Use them.

## 2. Submit; Then Stand

James 4:7 gives the divine order:

> *Therefore submit to God. But resist the devil, and he will flee from you.*

You can't resist what you haven't first submitted to G-d. Obedience is the doorway to authority. Submission is not weakness—it is spiritual alignment. And once we are aligned, the devil has no choice but to flee.

Resistance without submission is religion. But resistance through obedience is warfare—and the outcome is already sealed.

## 3. The Cross Disarmed the Enemy

Colossians 2:15 reveals the triumph of Calvary:

> *After disarming the principalities and powers, He made a public spectacle of them, triumphing over them in the cross.*

Satan is not ruling—he is already disarmed.

What was once a throne of torment has been replaced by a throne of triumph. Yeshua publicly shamed every dark power. Their schemes are now rooted in illusion and fear, not in actual power.

So why do we sometimes still feel bound? Because we haven't yet stood in what's already ours. Redemption brings peace, and peace silences fear.

## 4. Power, Love, and a Sound Mind

2 Timothy 1:7 (NKJV) declares plainly:

> *For God has not given us a spirit of fear, but of power and love and of a sound mind.*

You have been given a different spirit—power to confront darkness, love to drive out fear, and a sound mind to discern what is true.

When fear comes, speak the truth back to it:

- "I have authority."
- "I have power."
- "I have peace."
- "I have the name of Jesus of Nazareth."

Declare it until it takes root in your soul.

## 5. Overcoming by Blood and Testimony

Revelation 12:11 offers the keys to victory:

> *They overcame him by the blood of the Lamb and by the word of their testimony, and they did not love their lives even in the face of death.*

Victory is not a future possibility—it's a past and present event. And the blood of the Lamb has sealed it forever.

But your testimony makes it personal. Speak it. Live it. Stand in it. You don't overcome fear by silence—you overcome it by proclamation.

Declare what G-d has done. Say it out loud. Let every demon in hell know that you know who you are—and whose you are.

## Faith Cancels Fear

Faith doesn't pretend the storm isn't real—it just refuses to let the storm dictate the outcome.

Fear says, "What if it goes wrong?"

Faith says, "When G-d shows up …"

Fear says, "You're not enough."

Faith says, "He is more than enough."

Faith is the sword of peace. And when wielded, fear must flee.

You've been given divine tools. Use them. Walk in what was paid for.

## Declare: I Am Free

I am a victor in Christ.

I am not fighting for victory—Jesus has already won.

Fear has no hold on me.

I have been given divine authority, power, love, and a sound mind.

I rebuke fear and every lie of the enemy.

I stand in the Word. I walk in freedom.

I live in resurrection power.

I pray in the mighty name of Jesus of Nazareth—the Name above every name.

Amen.

## Closing Reflection

Peace and freedom walk hand in hand. The moment you let go of fear, you make room for peace. Not peace from this world, but peace from above. The kind that steadies the heart, anchors the soul, and silences the accuser.

You are not weak. You are not forgotten. You are not forsaken.

You are redeemed—through peace.

Now live like it.

# Closing Words

Shalom Aleichem

Peace, to you! 🕊

By Al Ezra

As this book draws to a close, may the words of the Messiah Himself remain with you:

> *"Take My yoke upon you and learn from Me, for I am gentle and humble in heart, and you will find rest for your souls. For My yoke is easy and My burden is light."*
>
> —Matthew 11:29-30

You were never meant to carry the weight of this world alone. His peace is your portion. His presence is your rest. His yoke is not heavy—it is healing.

## Daily Devotion to Peace

Let these simple truths become your daily practice. Every day, every moment, peace is within reach.

Read the Word – hide it in your heart. Let it shape your mind.

- Listen to the Word – hear the voice of your Shepherd guiding you.
- Say the Word – speak life. Speak truth. Speak peace aloud.
- Pray in the Name of Jesus – not as ritual, but as relationship.
- Worship in your heart – whether you are moving or still, He is near.

And when you pray, remember His instruction:

> *"But you, when you pray, go into your inner room ... and your Father, who sees in secret, will reward you."*
>
> —Matthew 6:6

## A Grateful and Watchful Heart

Above all, thank the Lord for everything.

Gratitude protects your peace. Thanksgiving silences complaint. And the humble heart is always the resting place of the Spirit.

Pray also with me:

> *"That you may be counted worthy to escape all these things that are about to happen, and to stand before the Son of Man."*
>
> —Luke 21:36

This was the instruction of Jesus—not just to watch the signs, but to pray with urgency and walk in holiness. **Ask that your name be found written in the Lamb's Book of Life.**

Because peace is not only for today—it is your path to eternity.

Shalom Aleichem.

*"Peace be upon you!"*

These are the words of Jesus.

Baruch ADONAI

AL EZRA

Redeemed Through Peace

The End.

# About the Author

Al Ezra is a faith-driven author, teacher, and storyteller whose works explore the intersection of Scripture, spiritual restoration, and divine truth. Rooted in the Word and led by the *Ruach Ha-Kodesh*, his writings call readers back to the heart of G-d with urgency, clarity, and compassion.

Al Ezra's calling is directed by EL ELYON "G-d MOST HIGH." It blends prophetic insight with simple devotion, always pointing toward the redemptive work of Yeshua of Nazareth—the Messiah. Whether addressing adults or children, the seeker or the seasoned believer, the words inspired by *The Ruach* carry a single aim: to reveal peace through the Person of Jesus.

Al Ezra is also the author of *Unless, Calling Man Back, Unless Someone Guides Me, The American Babylon,* and *Cleopas.* These together with *The Story of the Resurrection,* a film by Al Ezra, are all part of an unfolding journey of faith-based teaching and storytelling.

He signs off each message with this blessing inspired by Jesus:

"Peace, to you! "

Because in the end, that's what the redeemed walk in.

# Glossary

## Adonai –

A reverential title used for G-d in Hebrew, meaning "Lord." Often used in place of YHVH (the sacred name of G-d)

## Abide –

To remain or stay connected. In Scripture, it refers to staying in close relationship with Jesus (John 15).

## Authority (Spiritual) –

The delegated power believers receive through Jesus to stand against evil, speak the truth, and walk in freedom (Luke 10:19).

## Blood of the Lamb –

A reference to the sacrificial death of Jesus (Yeshua) on the cross. His blood redeems, forgives, and cleanses (Revelation 12:11).

## Confession –

The act of speaking truth in agreement with G-d's Word. In Scripture, confession often precedes forgiveness and freedom.

## Cross –

The instrument of Jesus' crucifixion. It represents both suffering and the victory of redemption for believers (Colossians 2:15).

## Fear (Spirit of) –

Described as a demonic influence used by the enemy to control, deceive, or paralyze. Countered by faith and truth (2 Timothy 1:7)

## Fruit of the Spirit –

The characteristics produced in a believer's life through the Holy Spirit, including peace, love, and joy (Galatians 5:22-23)

## Gethsemane –

The garden where Jesus prayed before His arrest. A place of deep surrender and peace under pressure (Luke 22:39-46).

## Messiah (Yeshua) –

The anointed one promised in Scripture, fulfilled in Jesus Christ. Yeshua is His Hebrew name, meaning "salvation"

## Peace (Shalom) –

More than the absence of conflict, shalom means wholeness, harmony, and divine rest. A gift and promise from G-d (Isaiah 26:3)

## Peacemaker –

One who actively brings reconciliation and unity through the Spirit of G-d. Peacemakers reflect the heart of Jesus (Matthew 5:9).

## Prayer Closet –

A term from Matthew 6:6 encouraging private, personal prayer in quiet solitude before G-d.

## Prince of Peace –

A prophetic title for Jesus found in Isaiah 9:6, emphasizing His role as the source and ruler of divine peace

## Redemption –

The act of being rescued, purchased, or restored by G-d through the sacrifice of Jesus. It brings both freedom and peace.

## Resist the Devil –

A command to actively stand against the enemy's tactics through submission to G-d and use of His Word (James 4:7)

## Ruach Ha-Kodesh –

Hebrew for "The Holy Spirit," the divine presence of G-d dwelling in and empowering believers

## Shalom Aleichem –

A traditional Hebrew greeting meaning "Peace be upon you." Also used as a farewell blessing in this book

## Testimony –

A spoken or written declaration of what G-d has done in a person's life. A powerful weapon against fear and doubt (Revelation 12:11)

## Yoke –

A symbol of submission and partnership. Jesus' yoke is easy and His burden is light, offering rest for the soul (Matthew 11:29-30).

# Glossary (with Hebrew Pronunciation)

## Adonai (Ah-doh-NAI) –

A reverential title for G-d in Hebrew, meaning "Lord." Used to respectfully address or reference the sacred name of G-d (YHVH)

## Abide –

To remain or stay connected. In Scripture, it refers to deep spiritual union with Jesus—resting, walking, and living in Him (John 15).

## Authority (Spiritual) –

The divine right and power given to believers through Jesus to speak, act, and stand in victory over evil (Luke 10:19)

## Blood of the Lamb –

The sacrificial blood of Jesus (Yeshua), which redeems, cleanses, and protects believers (Revelation 12:11)

## Confession –

The act of declaring truth and aligning your words with G-d's Word. Often connected to repentance and spiritual freedom

## Cross –

The means of Jesus' death and the symbol of redemption, victory, and sacrificial love (Colossians 2:15)

## Fear (Spirit of) –

A demonic spirit that opposes faith and peace. G-d did not give us a spirit of fear, but of power, love, and a sound mind (2 Timothy 1:7)

## Fruit of the Spirit –

Spiritual characteristics developed in the life of a believer by the Ruach Ha-Kodesh. Includes love, joy, peace, patience, etc. (Galatians 5:22-23)

## Gethsemane (Geth-SEM-uh-nee) –

The garden where Jesus prayed before His crucifixion. A place of surrender, suffering, and peace under pressure

## Messiah (Yeshua) (Yeh-SHOO-ah) –

The anointed one prophesied in the Hebrew Scriptures. Yeshua is the original Hebrew name of Jesus and means "Salvation"

## Peace (Shalom) (Sha-LOME) –

A rich Hebrew word meaning wholeness, safety, harmony, and divine well-being. Not just absence of conflict, but presence of G-d

## Peacemaker –

A person who carries and cultivates G-d's peace—bringing reconciliation, healing, and truth (Matthew 5:9)

## Prayer Closet –

A term from Matthew 6:6 referring to private, sincere, and undistracted communion with G-d

## Prince of Peace –

One of Jesus' titles from Isaiah 9:6, emphasizing His role as the bringer and ruler of everlasting peace

## Redemption –

The act of being purchased, rescued, or restored through the blood of Jesus. Brings peace, purpose, and new identity

## Resist the Devil –

To stand firm against temptation and spiritual attacks by submitting to G-d and speaking His truth (James 4:7)

## Ruach Ha-Kodesh (Roo-AHK Ha-KOH-desh) –

Hebrew for "The Holy Spirit." The divine Spirit of G-d who indwells, empowers, and sanctifies believers

## Shalom Aleichem (Sha-LOME Ah-LEH-khem) –

Hebrew greeting meaning "Peace be upon you." Often used as a blessing and farewell—Jesus spoke this to His disciples after His resurrection

# Notes

......................................................................................
......................................................................................
......................................................................................
......................................................................................
......................................................................................
......................................................................................
......................................................................................
......................................................................................
......................................................................................
......................................................................................
......................................................................................
......................................................................................
......................................................................................
......................................................................................
......................................................................................
......................................................................................
......................................................................................
......................................................................................
......................................................................................
......................................................................................

# Redeemed
## through Peace

# Redeemed
## through Peace

# Redeemed
## through Peace

# Redeemed
## through Peace

# Redeemed
## through Peace